# YOUR COMPLETE LIBRA 2024 PERSONAL HOROSCOPE

Monthly Astrological Prediction Forecast Readings of Every Zodiac Astrology Sun Star Signs- Love, Romance, Money, Finances, Career, Health, Travel, Spirituality.

Iris Quinn

Alpha Zuriel Publishing

Copyright © 2023 by **Iris Quinn**

All rights reserved. No part of this publication may be reproduced, distributed or transmitted in any form or by any means, without prior written permission.

**Alpha Zuriel Publishing**
**United States.**

The content contained within this book may not be reproduced, duplicated or transmitted without direct written permission from the author or the publisher.
Under no circumstances will any blame or legal responsibility be held against the publisher, or author, for any damages, reparation, or monetary loss due to the information contained within this book; either directly or indirectly.

Legal Notice:
This book is copyright protected. This book is only for personal use. You cannot amend, distribute, sell, use, quote or paraphrase any part, or the content within this book, without the consent of the author or publisher.

Disclaimer Notice:
Please note the information contained within this document is for educational and entertainment purposes only. All effort has been executed to present accurate, up to date, and reliable, complete information. No warranties of any kind are declared or implied. Readers acknowledge that the author is not engaging in the rendering of legal, financial, medical or professional advice.

**Your Complete Libra 2024 Personal Horoscope/ Iris Quinn**. -- 1st ed.

*"In the dance of the planets, we find the rhythms of life. Astrology reminds us that we are all connected to the greater universe, and our actions have ripple effects throughout the cosmos."*
— IRIS QUINN

# CONTENTS

LIBRA PROFILE .................................................... 7
PERSONALITY OF LIBRA ............................... 11
WEAKNESSES OF LIBRA ............................... 13
RELATIONSHIP COMPATIBILITY WITH LIBRA ................................................................. 15
LOVE AND PASSION ....................................... 23
MARRIAGE ........................................................ 25
LIBRA 2024 HOROSCOPE ................................ 28
   Overview Libra 2024 ......................................... 28
   January 2024 ..................................................... 32
   February 2024 ................................................... 39
   March 2024 ........................................................ 46
   April 2024 .......................................................... 53
   May 2024 ........................................................... 60
   June 2024 ........................................................... 67
   July 2024 ........................................................... 73
   August 2024 ...................................................... 79
   September 2024 ................................................. 85
   October 2024 ..................................................... 90
   November 2024 ................................................. 96
   December 2024 ................................................ 102

## CHAPTER ONE

# LIBRA PROFILE

- Constellation: Libra
- Zodiac Symbol: The Scales
- Date: September 23 - October 22
- Element: Air
- Ruling Planet: Venus
- Career Planet: Saturn
- Love Planet: Venus
- Money Planet: Venus
- Planet of Fun, Entertainment, Creativity, and Speculations: Sun
- Planet of Health and Work: Mercury
- Planet of Home and Family Life: Moon
- Planet of Spirituality: Neptune
- Planet of Travel, Education, Religion, and Philosophy: Jupiter

Colors:
- Colors: Light Blue, Pink

- Colors that promote love, romance, and social harmony: Pink, Lavender
- Color that promotes earning power: Green

- Gem: Opal
- Metals: Copper, Bronze
- Scent: Rose
- Birthstone: Opal

Libra Qualities:
- Quality: Cardinal (Represents leadership and initiative)
- Quality most needed for balance: Decisiveness.

Libra Virtues:
- Harmony
- Diplomacy
- Fairness
- Cooperation
- Social Grace

Deepest Need: Balance and Harmony

Characteristics to Embrace:
- Fairness and Justice

# 9 · COMPLETE LIBRA 2024 PERSONAL HOROSCOPE

- Charm and Grace
- Ability to see multiple perspectives.
- Negotiation and Compromise

Signs of Greatest Overall Compatibility:
- Gemini
- Aquarius

Signs of Greatest Overall Incompatibility:
- Cancer
- Capricorn

- Sign Most Supportive for Career Advancement: Capricorn
- Sign Most Supportive for Emotional Well-being: Cancer
- Sign Most Supportive Financially: Taurus
- Sign Best for Marriage and/or Partnerships: Libra
- Sign Most Supportive for Creative Projects: Leo
- Best Sign to Have Fun With: Leo

Signs Most Supportive in Spiritual Matters:
- Sagittarius
- Pisces

Best Day of the Week: Friday

## LIBRA TRAITS

- Charming and socially adept
- Diplomatic and skilled at finding compromises.
- Balanced and fair-minded
- Romantic and relationship-oriented
- Indecisive and prone to procrastination
- People-pleasing and conflict-avoidant
- Appreciative of beauty and aesthetics

## PERSONALITY OF LIBRA

The personality of Libra is characterized by their charming and diplomatic nature. They possess a natural ability to connect with others and create harmonious relationships. Libras are known for their refined taste and appreciation for beauty in all aspects of life. They have a strong sense of justice and fairness, always striving to create balance and equality. Libras are skilled peacemakers, adept at finding compromises and resolving conflicts in a harmonious manner. They have a deep appreciation for art, culture, and intellectual pursuits. However, Libras can sometimes struggle with decision-making, as they weigh all perspectives and seek to please everyone involved. They value relationships and prioritize maintaining harmonious connections with others. Libras are social beings who thrive in social settings, enjoying engaging conversations and building connections with diverse individuals. They are excellent listeners and have a natural ability to understand and empathize with others. Libras also have a strong sense of aesthetics and seek beauty and refinement in their surroundings. They have a keen eye for detail and strive to create an aesthetically pleasing environment. Overall, Libras are charismatic, diplomatic, and seek to create harmony and balance in all aspects of their lives.

## WEAKNESSES OF LIBRA

Libras have a few weaknesses that can affect their personality and relationships. One of their main weaknesses is their indecisiveness. Libras have a natural inclination to weigh all the options and consider every perspective before making a decision. While this can be a valuable trait, it can also lead to a tendency to overthink and struggle with making timely choices. Their desire for balance and harmony can often make them hesitant to take a stand or make firm decisions, as they fear upsetting the equilibrium.

Another weakness of Libras is their strong need for approval and their inclination to seek validation from others. They place a high value on maintaining positive relationships and can be overly concerned with how others perceive them. This desire for approval can lead to a tendency to people-please and put the needs and desires of others before their own. They may struggle with setting boundaries and asserting themselves, as they fear rejection or conflict.

Libras' aversion to conflict and their desire for peace can also be a weakness. They may avoid confrontations or difficult conversations, opting for harmony over addressing issues directly. This can result in unresolved tensions and a buildup of resentment over time. Their preference for avoiding conflicts can sometimes lead to passive-aggressive behavior or the tendency to sweep problems under the rug rather than addressing them head-on.

Additionally, Libras' pursuit of fairness and justice can sometimes make them indecisive, as they strive to find the most equitable solution for everyone involved. They may struggle with making choices that may upset others or disrupt the status quo, even if it is necessary for their own growth or well-being.

Overall, the weaknesses of Libra revolve around their indecisiveness, people-pleasing nature, avoidance of conflict, and their strong desire for approval and harmony in their relationships.

# RELATIONSHIP COMPATIBILITY WITH LIBRA

Based only on their Sun signs, this is how Libra interacts with others. These are the compatibility interpretations for all 12 potential Libra combinations. This is a limited and insufficient method of determining compatibility.

However, Sun-sign compatibility remains the foundation for overall harmony in a relationship.

The general rule is that yin and yang do not get along. Yin complements yin, and yang complements yang. While yin and yang partnerships can be successful, they require more effort. Earth and water zodiac signs are both Yin. Yang is represented by the fire and air zodiac signs.

Libra (Yin) and Aries (Yang)

When Libra (Yin) and Aries (Yang) come together, their energies create a dynamic and balanced relationship. Libra's harmonious nature seeks balance and compromise, while Aries brings passion and assertiveness. Their connection is built on mutual admiration and respect for each other's strengths. They can learn from each other's contrasting qualities and find a middle ground that allows for both independence and compromise.

Libra (Yin) and Taurus (Yin)

In a relationship between Libra (Yin) and Taurus (Yin), their shared Yin energy creates a stable and harmonious partnership. Both signs value security, loyalty, and the comforts of life. They work together to create a cozy and peaceful home environment. While they may encounter challenges when it comes to change and adaptability, their commitment to each other and shared values can help them overcome any obstacles.

Libra (Yin) and Gemini (Yang)

Libra (Yin) and Gemini (Yang) share a dynamic and intellectually stimulating relationship. Libra's harmonious nature complements Gemini's curiosity and versatility. They enjoy engaging in deep conversations and exploring new ideas together.

However, they may need to find a balance between Libra's need for stability and Gemini's changeable nature. With effective communication and compromise, they can maintain a harmonious and mentally stimulating relationship.

Libra (Yin) and Cancer (Yin)

In a relationship between Libra (Yin) and Cancer (Yin), their shared Yin energy fosters emotional depth and understanding. Both signs value harmony, love, and emotional connections. They have a natural ability to empathize with each other's feelings and create a nurturing environment. However, they may need to navigate challenges related to decision-making and compromise. With open communication and mutual support, they can cultivate a loving and compassionate partnership.

Libra (Yin) and Leo (Yang)

When Libra (Yin) and Leo (Yang) join forces, their energies create a vibrant and social relationship. Libra's diplomatic nature blends well with Leo's confidence and charisma. They enjoy indulging in the finer things in life and can create a luxurious and stylish lifestyle together. However, they may need to balance their individual desires for attention and recognition. With mutual admiration and respect, they can build a strong and mutually beneficial partnership.

Libra (Yin) and Virgo (Yang)

In a relationship between Libra (Yin) and Virgo (Yang), their energies can complement each other. Libra's social skills and charm can balance Virgo's practicality and attention to detail. They have the potential to create a harmonious and organized life together. However, they may need to work on communication and finding common ground, as Virgo's critical nature can sometimes clash with Libra's desire for peace. With patience and understanding, they can develop a stable and supportive partnership.

Libra (Yin) and Libra (Yin)

When two Libra individuals come together, their shared Yin energy creates a relationship built on harmony, balance, and mutual understanding. They both value peace, justice, and aesthetics, creating a harmonious and aesthetically pleasing life together. However, they may need to be mindful of indecisiveness and overthinking, as both individuals strive to maintain balance and avoid conflicts. With open communication and a willingness to compromise, they can create a harmonious and fulfilling partnership.

Libra (Yin) and Scorpio (Yang)

In a relationship between Libra (Yin) and Scorpio (Yang), their energies can create a powerful and transformative connection. Libra's desire for balance and harmony can complement Scorpio's intensity and depth. They have the potential to delve into deep emotional connections and create a passionate and meaningful partnership. However, they may need to navigate issues related to trust and control. With open communication and mutual respect, they can build a strong and transformative relationship.

Libra (Yin) and Sagittarius (Yang)

When Libra (Yin) and Sagittarius (Yang) come together, their energies create an adventurous and intellectually stimulating relationship. Libra's love for harmony blends well with Sagittarius' optimism and love for exploration. They enjoy sharing experiences, traveling, and engaging in philosophical discussions. However, they may need to find a balance between Libra's desire for stability and Sagittarius' need for freedom. With open-mindedness and mutual support, they can cultivate a relationship filled with growth and adventure.

Libra (Yin) and Capricorn (Yang)

In a relationship between Libra (Yin) and Capricorn (Yang), their energies can create a balanced and complementary partnership. Libra's social grace and diplomacy can harmonize with Capricorn's ambition and practicality. They can work together to achieve goals and create a stable and secure life. However, they may need to navigate differences in priorities and approach to life. With patience and compromise, they can build a solid and successful partnership.

Libra (Yin) and Aquarius (Yang)

When Libra (Yin) and Aquarius (Yang) join forces, their energies create a unique and intellectually stimulating relationship. Libra's love for harmony aligns well with Aquarius' innovative and independent nature. They enjoy engaging in intellectual conversations, exploring new ideas, and supporting each other's individuality. However, they may need to find a balance between Libra's desire for balance and Aquarius' need for personal freedom. With open communication and respect for each other's individuality, they can build a relationship that promotes growth and intellectual stimulation.

Libra (Yin) and Pisces (Yin)

In a relationship between Libra (Yin) and Pisces (Yin), their shared Yin energy creates a compassionate and emotionally sensitive connection. Both signs value harmony, love, and emotional depth. They have a natural ability to understand and support each other's emotions. However, they may need to navigate challenges related to decision-making and practicality. With open communication and a strong emotional connection, they can create a loving and spiritually fulfilling partnership.

## LOVE AND PASSION

When it comes to love and passion, Libra individuals are the epitome of grace and romance. They have a deep appreciation for beauty, harmony, and the finer things in life, and this is reflected in their approach to love.

Libras are natural lovers and seek balance and equality in their relationships. They have a captivating charm and a magnetic personality that draws others towards them. They are experts at creating a romantic atmosphere, whether it's through thoughtful gestures, enchanting dates, or heartfelt conversations.

Passion runs through the veins of Libra, and they believe in the power of love to transform and elevate their lives. They are deeply attuned to their partner's needs and desires, and they strive to create a sense of harmony and mutual understanding in their relationships.

Libras value fairness and justice, and this extends to their approach to love. They believe in open communication, compromise, and finding common ground with their partner. They are skilled diplomats and mediators, always seeking a peaceful resolution in conflicts.

In love, Libras are committed and devoted partners. They prioritize the happiness and well-being of their loved ones, and they are willing to go to great lengths to ensure the success of their relationships. They thrive in partnerships where there is mutual respect, intellectual stimulation, and a strong emotional connection.

For Libras, love is a work of art, and they approach it with creativity, elegance, and a desire for lasting harmony. They understand the importance of maintaining the spark of passion in their relationships and continuously strive to deepen the emotional and physical connection with their partner.

In essence, Libras bring a sense of beauty, balance, and harmony to their love lives. Their passionate nature, combined with their commitment to fairness and equality, makes them extraordinary partners who create a love story that is both enchanting and enduring.

# MARRIAGE

Marriage for Libra is a significant and meaningful commitment that they approach with thoughtfulness and a desire for harmony. While they are generally supportive of the institution of marriage, there are certain aspects they consider before taking the plunge.

Financial stability is important to Libras before entering into marriage. They believe in creating a secure foundation for their future together, and they want to ensure that their financial position is solid before making such a commitment. This allows them to provide for their partner and build a life of comfort and security.

However, Libras need to be mindful of their tendency to engage in disputes and criticism. In order to maintain a healthy and thriving marriage, they must learn to temper their inclination to nitpick and argue. By fostering open and respectful communication, they can avoid weakening their partner's morale and jeopardizing the overall relationship.

Libras are dedicated to keeping their marriage alive and vibrant. They are willing to put in the effort and work required to maintain a harmonious partnership. However, if they feel that the disagreements and challenges become insurmountable, they will not hesitate to consider ending the marriage. They value their own happiness and understand the importance of being in a relationship that brings them fulfillment and peace.

In marriage, Libra women showcase their adaptability and ability to balance work and family responsibilities. They strive for order and efficiency, ensuring that tasks related to marriage and family life are done with dedication and a positive attitude. They take pride in creating a harmonious home environment where both partners feel supported and valued.

Libra men, on the other hand, are dedicated and hardworking individuals who prioritize their roles as husbands and fathers. They reject sexism and are committed to equality within their relationships. They believe in sharing responsibilities and ensuring that their spouse is not burdened with more than their fair share. They aim to create a partnership based on mutual respect and collaboration.

Overall, marriage for Libra is a commitment they take seriously. They strive for balance, harmony, and fairness in their relationships. By addressing financial stability, managing their tendencies for disputes, and fostering a supportive and equal partnership, Libras can create a fulfilling and enduring marriage that brings them joy and satisfaction.

CHAPTER TWO

# LIBRA 2024 HOROSCOPE

## Overview Libra 2024

The year 2024 promises to be a year of growth and transformation for Libra. The planetary movements indicate a year filled with opportunities and challenges that will push you to evolve and grow in all aspects of your life. The year will be marked by significant planetary aspects involving Mars, Mercury, Venus, and Jupiter, which will influence your career, relationships, health, and personal development.

The year 2024 will be a year of progress and expansion in your career. The presence of Mars in

Taurus in June indicates a time of hard work and perseverance. You may face some obstacles, but your determination will help you overcome them. The semi-sextile aspect between Mars and Jupiter in Gemini suggests opportunities for growth and expansion in your career. You may find yourself taking on new responsibilities or embarking on new projects.

In September, the trine aspect between Venus in Libra and Jupiter in Gemini indicates a time of financial prosperity. You may receive financial rewards for your hard work, or you may find opportunities for financial growth. However, the square aspect between Sun in Virgo and Jupiter in Gemini in September suggests a need for careful financial planning. Avoid impulsive spending and make sure to save for the future.

The year 2024 will be a year of deepening relationships and expanding social connections. The conjunction between Mercury and Venus in Cancer in June suggests a time of emotional communication in your relationships. You may find yourself expressing your feelings more openly, leading to deeper connections with your loved ones.

In August, the square aspect between Venus in Leo and Uranus in Taurus suggests a time of change and unpredictability in your social life. You may meet new people who challenge your views and push you to grow. Embrace these changes and learn from the experiences they bring.

The year 2024 will be a year of focus on health and wellness. The quincunx aspect between Sun in Cancer and Pluto in Aquarius in June suggests a need to balance your physical health with your mental and emotional well-being. Make sure to take time for self-care and relaxation.

In May, the semi-sextile aspect between Mars in Aries and Uranus in Taurus suggests a time of increased energy and vitality. Use this energy to focus on your physical health and wellness. Engage in regular exercise and maintain a balanced diet to ensure your well-being.

The year 2024 will be a year of spiritual growth and personal development. The quintile aspect between Jupiter and Saturn in May suggests a time of learning and growth. You may find yourself drawn to spiritual or philosophical studies that help you understand yourself and the world around you better.

In June, the square aspect between Venus in Cancer and True Node in Aries suggests a time of self-discovery. You may find yourself questioning your values and beliefs, leading to a deeper understanding of who you are and what you want from life.

The year 2024 will be a transformative year for Libra. The planetary movements indicate a year filled with opportunities for growth in all aspects of your life. Embrace the challenges and opportunities that come your way and use them to evolve and grow. Remember, the key to navigating this year successfully is balance - balance in your career and finances, balance in your relationships and social life, and balance in your health and wellness. With balance and perseverance, you can make the most of the opportunities that 2024 brings.

# January 2024

### Horoscope

Dear Libra, as you step into the month of January 2024, the celestial configurations encourage you to focus on establishing balance and harmony in all areas of your life. This is a time of self-reflection and introspection, allowing you to make necessary adjustments and find inner peace. Your natural diplomacy and ability to see both sides of a situation will be highly valued during this period.

The month begins with Venus squaring Saturn on January 1st, indicating potential challenges or responsibilities within your relationships. It's important to approach these hurdles with patience and open communication. By addressing any issues directly, you can foster understanding and find constructive solutions.

In summary, January offers opportunities for growth and self-discovery for Libra. Embrace the need for balance, harmony, and practicality in various aspects of your life. By maintaining a holistic approach to your well-being and relationships, you will align yourself with the cosmic energies and find fulfillment in the journey ahead.

Love

In matters of the heart, January presents a mix of energies for Libra. The square between Venus and Saturn on January 1st may introduce challenges or responsibilities within your relationships. Patience and open communication are key to navigating these obstacles. It's important to approach these hurdles with grace and a willingness to find mutually beneficial solutions. However, on January 3rd, the quincunx aspect between Venus and Jupiter suggests the potential for growth and expansion in your love life. This alignment encourages you to explore new possibilities and embrace positive changes within your relationships. It's a favorable time to address any issues or concerns, as well as to express your desires and needs openly. By engaging in open and honest conversations, you can strengthen the foundations of your partnerships. Additionally, on January 11th, the trine between Venus and Chiron fosters healing and emotional connection. This alignment offers an opportunity to work through past wounds and enhance intimacy within your relationships. It's a time for vulnerability and emotional support, allowing you and your partner to deepen your connection on a soul level. Be open to receiving and giving love, as this alignment can bring profound healing and growth. Throughout January, it's important to maintain a balanced approach in your relationships. Communicate with clarity, kindness, and empathy, as Mercury's quintile with Saturn on January 3rd emphasizes the need for clear and practical conversations. By actively listening and considering the perspectives of others, you can create a harmonious and loving atmosphere.

Career

January brings a focus on your career, Libra. The biquintile aspect between Venus and Jupiter on January 8th presents opportunities for professional growth and recognition. Your charm and diplomacy will play a significant role in creating positive impressions and building important connections with colleagues and superiors. This alignment emphasizes the importance of networking and leveraging your interpersonal skills to advance your career. However, it's crucial to maintain a practical approach and avoid being overly idealistic, as the square between Mercury and Neptune on the same day may cloud your judgment. By staying grounded and focusing on realistic goals, you can make the most of the opportunities that come your way. Trust your instincts and rely on your natural ability to balance multiple perspectives.

Finance

In January, your financial matters require careful attention, Libra. The semi-square aspect between Venus and Pluto on January 10th urges you to exercise caution when it comes to money matters. Avoid impulsive spending and prioritize long-term financial security over short-term gratification. This is a time for responsible budgeting and wise financial decisions. Consider seeking professional advice or educating yourself about investment strategies to make informed choices. The alignment of Mercury's square with Neptune on January 8th serves as a reminder to be vigilant and avoid falling for deceptive financial schemes. Trust your intuition and conduct thorough research before making any significant financial commitments. By adopting a practical and disciplined approach to your finances, you can lay a solid foundation for long-term prosperity.

### Health

Your health and well-being are of utmost importance in January, Libra. The semi-square aspect between the Sun and Saturn on January 9th serves as a gentle reminder to prioritize self-care. Establishing a regular exercise routine, maintaining a balanced diet, and getting sufficient rest are essential for maintaining your physical and mental well-being. This is a favorable time to incorporate stress management techniques, such as meditation or yoga, into your daily routine. Additionally, the trine between the Sun and Uranus on January 9th encourages you to explore alternative healing modalities and embrace innovative approaches to your health. Be open to trying new wellness practices that resonate with your unique needs. Trust your intuition and listen to the messages your body sends you. Taking care of your health will enable you to approach other areas of your life with energy and vitality.

### Travel

January brings opportunities for travel and exploration, Libra. The quintile aspect between Mars and Neptune on January 22nd sparks your sense of adventure and encourages you to embark on new journeys. Whether it's a short getaway or a longer expedition, travel can bring inspiration, broaden your horizons, and provide a fresh perspective. Embrace the opportunity to explore different cultures, traditions, and landscapes. It's a time for personal growth and expanding your worldview. However, it's important to plan your trips carefully and be mindful of any potential disruptions or delays that may arise. Stay flexible and open to unexpected changes in your travel plans. Use your diplomatic skills to navigate any challenges that may occur during your journeys. Remember to take time for self-reflection and relaxation during your travels. Embrace the opportunity to disconnect from your daily routine and immerse yourself in new experiences. Whether you're traveling for leisure or business, it's a time to find joy in discovering new places and creating lasting memories.

Insight from the stars

As you navigate January, Libra, the stars encourage you to embrace balance, harmony, and practicality. This is a time for self-reflection and making necessary adjustments to create a fulfilling life. Trust your diplomatic nature and ability to see both sides of a situation. By maintaining equilibrium and open communication, you can overcome any challenges and seize the opportunities that come your way. Embrace the transformative energy of the new year and use it to create a life filled with love, success, and well-being.

Best days of the month: January 8th, 11th, 12th, 19th, 23rd, 27th, and 29th.

# February 2024

## Horoscope

February brings a shift in energy for Libra, as you find yourself embracing deep introspection and self-reflection. The celestial aspects highlight the importance of inner harmony and personal growth during this month. It's a time for introspection, contemplation, and understanding your own needs and desires. Take the opportunity to reconnect with your inner self, reassess your goals, and make necessary adjustments to align with your authentic path. Embrace solitude and self-care practices that nourish your mind, body, and soul. This period of self-reflection will lay the foundation for a balanced and fulfilling life moving forward.

## Love

In matters of the heart, February brings a mix of energies for Libra. The square aspect between Venus and Chiron on February 5th may bring emotional challenges and the need for healing within relationships. It's essential to approach these difficulties with compassion and understanding. Allow yourself and your partner the space to express vulnerability and address any unresolved wounds. The sextile between Venus and True Node on February 6th offers opportunities for growth and soul connections. This alignment encourages you to align your romantic partnerships with your higher purpose. It's a favorable time to explore shared goals and envision a future together. However, the square between Venus and Jupiter on February 24th may bring some challenges related to balancing your personal desires with the needs of your relationships. It's important to find a harmonious compromise and avoid being overly indulgent or self-centered. Communication and open dialogue will be key in navigating these challenges. Embrace the transformative energy and use it as an opportunity to deepen your emotional connections and create a loving and supportive environment.

Career

In your professional life, February presents a favorable period for growth and advancement, Libra. The quintile aspect between Mercury and Jupiter on February 22nd enhances your communication skills and intellectual prowess. You'll find yourself able to articulate your ideas effectively and gain recognition for your contributions. It's a time to share your knowledge and collaborate with colleagues, as teamwork will lead to success. Embrace networking opportunities and seek feedback to refine your skills and expand your professional network. However, the semi-square aspect between Venus and Saturn on February 10th may introduce some challenges or responsibilities in your career. Stay focused, maintain a strong work ethic, and persevere through any obstacles that come your way. By demonstrating your dedication and reliability, you'll earn the respect and admiration of your superiors. It's also important to seek a healthy work-life balance during this time. Prioritize self-care and avoid overextending yourself. By taking care of your well-being, you'll have the energy and clarity of mind to excel in your professional endeavors.

Finance

February brings a focus on your financial matters, Libra. The semi-sextile aspect between Venus and Saturn on February 23rd reminds you of the importance of responsible financial planning. Take the time to review your budget, assess your expenses, and make necessary adjustments to ensure stability and security. It's a favorable time to seek professional advice or educate yourself about long-term investment strategies. Avoid impulsive spending and prioritize practicality and long-term financial goals. The sextile between Venus and True Node on February 29th may bring opportunities for financial growth and stability. Embrace these opportunities with a balanced approach, considering both risks and rewards. It's crucial to maintain a realistic perspective and avoid taking unnecessary financial risks. By practicing discipline and making sound financial decisions, you'll pave the way for long-term prosperity and abundance.

Health

In February, it's important for Libra to prioritize their health and well-being. The conjunction between the Sun and Mercury on February 28th amplifies your mental and physical energy. It's a favorable time to engage in physical activities that bring you joy and boost your overall vitality. Regular exercise routines, such as yoga or cardio workouts, will help you maintain a healthy balance. Pay attention to your emotional well-being as well, as the semi-square aspect between Mars and Neptune on February 28th may bring some emotional sensitivities. Engage in stress-relief practices, such as meditation or journaling, to maintain a balanced state of mind. Nurturing your emotional health will positively impact your physical well-being. Lastly, be mindful of your dietary choices. Incorporate nutritious foods into your meals, focusing on a well-rounded and balanced diet. Avoid excessive indulgence or emotional eating, as it may disrupt your overall health and energy levels. By prioritizing self-care and creating healthy habits, you'll enhance your well-being and approach life with a renewed sense of vitality.

Travel

February brings opportunities for travel and exploration, Libra. The conjunction between Venus and Mars on February 22nd sparks your sense of adventure and encourages you to embark on new journeys. Whether it's a spontaneous weekend getaway or a planned vacation, travel will provide you with fresh perspectives and new experiences. Embrace the opportunity to immerse yourself in different cultures, connect with diverse people, and broaden your horizons. It's a time for personal growth and expanding your worldview. However, it's essential to plan your trips carefully and be mindful of any potential disruptions or travel restrictions that may arise. Stay flexible and open to unexpected changes in your travel plans. Embrace the thrill of spontaneity while also being prepared for any unforeseen circumstances. Use your diplomatic skills to navigate any challenges that may occur during your journeys.

Insight from the stars

As you navigate February, Libra, the stars encourage you to embrace balance, adaptability, and perseverance. This is a time to trust your intuition and follow your heart's desires. Allow your inner wisdom to guide you in making decisions that align with your authentic self. Find harmony in your relationships, career, and personal well-being. Stay open to growth and transformation, as challenges and opportunities will shape your journey. Remember to nurture yourself, both physically and emotionally, as this will provide a solid foundation for success. Embrace the celestial energies and use them to manifest your dreams and create a life filled with love, abundance, and fulfillment.

Best days of the month: February 5th, 6th, 12th, 16th, 20th, 22nd, and 26th.

# March 2024

Horoscope

March brings a mix of transformative energies for Libra, encouraging you to embrace personal growth and self-discovery. The celestial aspects highlight the importance of balance, adaptability, and intuition. This is a time for deepening your understanding of yourself and your place in the world. Embrace the opportunities for personal transformation and take time for self-reflection and introspection. Trust your instincts and allow your intuition to guide you in making decisions that align with your authentic self. Stay open to the unexpected and be willing to adapt to changing circumstances. By maintaining a harmonious balance between your inner world and external experiences, you'll navigate this month with grace and create a solid foundation for future endeavors.

Love

In matters of the heart, March presents a dynamic mix of energies for Libra. The sextile aspect between

Venus and Chiron on March 2nd opens the door for deep emotional healing and understanding within relationships. It's a time to address any unresolved wounds and nurture emotional connections with compassion and empathy. The square aspect between Venus and Uranus on March 3rd may bring some challenges and disruptions in love. It's important to remain open-minded and flexible, as unexpected events or changes may require adaptation in your relationships. Use this period as an opportunity for growth and expansion, exploring new ways of connecting with your partner and finding innovative solutions to any conflicts that may arise. The conjunction between Venus and Saturn on March 21st brings stability and commitment to your relationships. It's a favorable time for long-term partnerships and making meaningful commitments. Embrace the responsibility and dedication required to nurture love and create a solid foundation for the future. Communication and open-heartedness will be essential in navigating the complexities of love during this transformative month.

## Career

In your professional life, March brings a focus on self-expression and creativity for Libra. The semi-sextile aspect between Mercury and Mars on March 1st enhances your communication skills and assertiveness. This alignment empowers you to express your ideas and opinions with confidence and clarity. It's a favorable time for presentations, negotiations, and collaborative projects. Embrace opportunities to share your unique perspective and contribute to team efforts. However, the conjunction between Mercury and Neptune on March 8th may bring some challenges in maintaining focus and clarity. Be mindful of potential miscommunications or misunderstandings and take extra care in reviewing details and instructions. The semi-sextile aspect between Mercury and Saturn on March 16th encourages you to approach your work with discipline and responsibility. Focus on tasks that require attention to detail and thoroughness. It's a time to establish a solid foundation for future success by adhering to deadlines and maintaining professionalism. The sextile aspect between Mercury and Pluto on March 28th enhances your problem-solving abilities and strategic thinking. Embrace this alignment to explore innovative solutions and make powerful connections in your professional endeavors. Overall, March offers opportunities for growth, self-expression, and strategic advancement in your career.

Finance

March highlights the importance of financial stability and responsible money management for Libra. The semi-sextile aspect between Venus and Saturn on March 12th reminds you to approach your finances with discipline and caution. It's a time to review your budget, assess your expenses, and make necessary adjustments to ensure long-term stability and security. Avoid impulsive spending and focus on practicality and wise investments. The conjunction between Venus and Saturn on March 21st strengthens your financial discipline and commitment to long-term goals. Embrace this alignment to create a solid foundation for your financial future. Seek professional advice or educate yourself about investment strategies that align with your goals. The sextile aspect between Venus and Jupiter on March 24th brings opportunities for financial growth and expansion. It's a favorable time to explore new avenues for income generation and consider long-term investments. However, remain cautious and carefully assess potential risks and rewards. Practice patience and avoid making hasty financial decisions. By maintaining a balanced approach to your finances, you'll lay the groundwork for stability and prosperity in the long run.

Health

The conjunction between Mercury and Neptune on March 8th encourages you to prioritize your emotional and mental health. Engage in mindfulness practices, meditation, or journaling to maintain a sense of inner calm and clarity. Pay attention to your intuitive insights and allow yourself time for introspection and self-reflection. The semi-square aspect between Mars and Chiron on March 27th may bring some emotional sensitivities. Take extra care to address any emotional wounds or stressors. Seek support from loved ones or consider professional guidance if needed. The semi-square aspect between the Sun and Pluto on March 21st reminds you to release any emotional baggage and embrace transformation. Let go of negative patterns or habits that may be affecting your well-being and embrace positive lifestyle changes. Nourish your body with healthy and nutritious foods, engage in regular exercise, and prioritize quality rest and sleep. Be mindful of your energy levels and avoid overexertion or burnout. Find a balance between work and personal life to maintain a harmonious and healthy lifestyle.

Travel

March presents opportunities for travel and exploration for Libra. The semi-sextile aspect between Mars and Neptune on March 19th ignites your sense of adventure and encourages you to seek new experiences. Embrace the opportunity to embark on spontaneous trips or plan a vacation to a destination that captivates your imagination. Travel will not only provide a break from your daily routine but also offer insights and inspiration. Immerse yourself in different cultures, connect with diverse people, and explore new horizons. It's a time to broaden your perspective and gain a deeper understanding of the world. However, be mindful of any potential travel restrictions or unforeseen circumstances that may impact your plans. Stay flexible and prepared to adapt to changing situations. Pack your sense of adventure and curiosity as you navigate new territories and create lasting memories. Embrace the joy of discovery and embrace the experiences that expand your horizons.

Insight from the stars

As you journey through March, Libra, the stars encourage you to embrace balance, self-expression, and responsible decision-making. This is a month of transformation and personal growth, calling for self-reflection and adaptability. Trust your intuition and inner wisdom as you navigate the complexities of love, career, finances, and health. Seek harmony within yourself and your relationships, and approach challenges with resilience and grace. Stay open to new experiences and be willing to adapt to unexpected circumstances. By aligning with the celestial energies, you'll navigate this transformative month with grace and create a path of growth and fulfillment.

Best days of the month: March 1st, 8th, 16th, 21st, 24th, 27th, and 28th

# April 2024

Horoscope

In April, Libra, the cosmic energies invite you to focus on self-expression, personal growth, and finding balance in various areas of your life. The conjunction between Mercury and Venus on April 2nd enhances your communication skills and brings harmony to your relationships. It's a favorable time for heartfelt conversations and resolving any conflicts or misunderstandings. The Sun's semi-sextile with Saturn on April 2nd encourages you to establish a sense of discipline and structure in your life. This will support your endeavors and help you achieve long-term goals. Embrace this month as an opportunity for self-reflection and introspection, as you seek to align your actions with your core values. Embrace your innate sense of fairness and find ways to bring harmony to your interactions and environment. By cultivating a balanced and authentic approach, you'll navigate April with grace and clarity.

Love

In matters of the heart, April brings opportunities for deepening emotional connections and enhancing intimacy for Libra. The conjunction between Venus and Neptune on April 3rd infuses your romantic encounters with a sense of magic and tenderness. It's a time to express your love and affection openly, creating a romantic atmosphere that nurtures the soul. Embrace your natural charm and communication skills to deepen emotional bonds with your partner. Single Libras may find themselves drawn to spiritual or compassionate individuals who resonate with their values. However, be mindful of any idealization or illusions that may cloud your judgment. The Sun's conjunction with Chiron on April 8th encourages healing within relationships. Use this energy to address any emotional wounds or past traumas that may be affecting your ability to fully connect with others. Practice open communication, empathy, and active listening to foster understanding and growth in your partnerships. Nurture your relationships through shared experiences, heartfelt conversations, and acts of kindness. Remember to also prioritize self-love and self-care, as this forms the foundation for healthy and balanced connections. By fostering emotional vulnerability and authenticity, you'll create a loving and harmonious space for love to thrive.

### Career

April presents opportunities for career growth and professional advancement for Libra. The sextile aspect between Mars and Jupiter on April 19th brings a surge of motivation and enthusiasm to pursue your ambitions. It's a favorable time to take calculated risks and explore new professional avenues. Trust your instincts and seize opportunities that align with your passions and long-term goals. The conjunction between Mercury and Venus on April 19th enhances your communication skills, making it an ideal time for networking, negotiations, and collaborative projects. Your ability to articulate your ideas and connect with others will propel you forward in your career. However, be mindful of the semi-square aspect between Venus and Saturn on April 30th, which may bring some challenges or delays in your professional endeavors. Practice patience and perseverance, and trust that your hard work will eventually pay off. Remain adaptable and open to learning opportunities, as they may lead to unexpected breakthroughs. Seek feedback from mentors or colleagues to refine your skills and broaden your knowledge. Embrace a proactive and determined mindset, and you'll make significant strides in your career during April.

Finance

April encourages Libra to adopt a practical and responsible approach to their finances. The semi-sextile aspect between Mercury and Saturn on April 16th emphasizes the importance of financial planning and disciplined budgeting. Take the time to assess your financial situation, set clear financial goals, and create a realistic budget that aligns with your long-term aspirations. The conjunction between Venus and Chiron on April 21st may bring some emotional triggers or past financial wounds to the surface. Use this energy as an opportunity to address any limiting beliefs or patterns that may hinder your financial growth. Seek guidance from a financial advisor or mentor to gain a fresh perspective on investment opportunities or strategies to increase your wealth. Remember to strike a balance between saving for the future and enjoying the present. Treat yourself occasionally but avoid impulsive purchases that may compromise your financial stability. Practice gratitude for the abundance in your life and cultivate a mindset of abundance and prosperity. With diligence, smart decision-making, and a balanced approach, you'll navigate April with financial stability and set a solid foundation for your future financial goals.

Health

In April, Libra's focus on self-care and overall well-being is highlighted. The semi-square aspect between Mars and Pluto on April 13th may bring intense energy and potential power struggles. Channel this energy into physical activities and exercise to release any tension and maintain emotional balance. Engage in activities that promote mental and emotional well-being, such as meditation, journaling, or spending time in nature. The Sun's conjunction with Mercury on April 11th enhances your mental clarity and cognitive abilities. Take advantage of this period to engage in stimulating activities that challenge your mind, such as puzzles, reading, or learning new skills. It's crucial to establish a harmonious work-life balance to avoid burnout. Set clear boundaries and prioritize self-care routines that nourish your mind, body, and soul. Ensure you're getting enough restorative sleep, as it plays a vital role in maintaining your overall health. If you've neglected any health concerns, address them promptly to prevent any further complications. Seek support from healthcare professionals or holistic practitioners to create a personalized wellness plan. Remember to listen to your body's signals and honor your needs.

### Travel

In April, Libra, the celestial energies encourage you to find balance within yourself and your relationships. The harmonious aspects between Venus, Mercury, and Neptune emphasize the importance of open communication, empathy, and compassion. Use this time to connect deeply with others, fostering harmonious connections and resolving any conflicts. The conjunction between the Sun and Chiron invites you to heal emotional wounds and embrace vulnerability, leading to personal growth and increased self-awareness. Trust your intuition and allow it to guide you in making decisions that align with your authentic self. Embrace the transformative power of the celestial energies, and you'll navigate April with grace and a heightened sense of inner harmony.

Insight from the stars

In April, Libra, the celestial energies encourage you to find balance within yourself and your relationships. The harmonious aspects between Venus, Mercury, and Neptune emphasize the importance of open communication, empathy, and compassion. Use this time to connect deeply with others, fostering harmonious connections and resolving any conflicts. The conjunction between the Sun and Chiron invites you to heal emotional wounds and embrace vulnerability, leading to personal growth and increased self-awareness. Trust your intuition and allow it to guide you in making decisions that align with your authentic self. Embrace the transformative power of the celestial energies, and you'll navigate April with grace and a heightened sense of inner harmony.

Best days of the month: April 2nd, 8th, 19th, 20th, 21st, 23rd and 28th.

# May 2024

Horoscope

In May, Libra, the celestial energies encourage you to focus on self-expression, communication, and personal growth. The square aspect between Venus and Pluto on May 1st may bring intensity and potential power struggles in your relationships. Use this energy as an opportunity to deepen your emotional connections and address any underlying issues. The Sun's semi-square with Neptune on May 3rd may create a sense of confusion or uncertainty. Take time to clarify your goals and aspirations, and trust your intuition to guide you in making important decisions. The conjunction between the Sun and Uranus on May 13th brings a wave of excitement and unexpected opportunities for personal growth and transformation. Embrace the change and step outside your comfort zone. Maintain balance and stability by nurturing your relationships and connecting with loved ones. Take time to listen and communicate openly to avoid misunderstandings. The celestial energies support personal and spiritual development, so engage in practices such as meditation, journaling, or exploring new philosophies. May is a month of growth, transformation, and finding harmony within yourself and your connections with others.

Love

The conjunction between Venus and Jupiter on May 23rd creates a harmonious and expansive energy in your relationships. This period offers opportunities for deepening emotional connections, growth, and shared adventures with your partner. Single Libras may experience a surge of romantic opportunities and meaningful connections during this time. Embrace new experiences and step out of your comfort zone to attract love into your life. The square aspect between Venus and Mars on May 29th may bring some challenges and potential conflicts. Use this energy as an opportunity for growth and increased understanding within your relationships. Practice active listening, empathy, and open communication to maintain harmony. The conjunction between Mars and Chiron on May 29th invites you to confront any wounds or insecurities within yourself or your relationships. Healing is possible by addressing these issues with compassion and understanding. Take time for self-reflection and self-care to nurture your emotional well-being.

## Career

May presents opportunities for professional growth and advancement for Libra. The conjunction between Mercury and Chiron on May 6th enhances your communication skills and ability to express yourself effectively in the workplace. Use this energy to share your ideas, collaborate with colleagues, and assert your opinions with confidence. The sextile between Venus and Saturn on May 13th supports stability and long-term success in your career endeavors. Focus on building solid foundations and implementing practical strategies to achieve your professional goals. The conjunction between the Sun and Uranus on May 13th brings unexpected opportunities for career growth and recognition. Embrace these moments of change and innovation, and be open to taking calculated risks. The trine aspect between the Sun and Pluto on May 22nd empowers you to tap into your personal power and make significant progress in your career. Trust your instincts and allow your ambitions to drive you forward. However, be mindful of potential power struggles or conflicts that may arise due to the square aspect between Mercury and Pluto on May 17th. Practice diplomacy, active listening, and finding common ground to resolve any conflicts that arise.

## Finance

May brings favorable financial opportunities and stability for Libra. The conjunction between Venus and Jupiter on May 23rd augments your financial abundance and opportunities for growth. This period may bring fortunate financial ventures, favorable negotiations, or unexpected windfalls. However, be cautious with overspending or making impulsive financial decisions, particularly during the square aspect between Venus and Mars on May 29th. It's essential to maintain a balanced approach and consider long-term financial goals. The sextile between Venus and Saturn on May 13th supports your financial stability and long-term investments. Consider implementing practical strategies to enhance your financial security and create a solid foundation for future endeavors. Stay organized, track your expenses, and seek expert advice if necessary. The trine aspect between the Sun and Pluto on May 22nd empowers you to make wise financial decisions and tap into your personal power to attract abundance. Focus on strategic planning and remain disciplined in managing your finances. Overall, May presents favorable financial prospects, but it's important to exercise caution, practice financial responsibility, and make informed decisions.

## Health

In May, Libra, it's important to prioritize your health and well-being. The conjunction between Mars and Chiron on May 29th highlights the significance of addressing any physical or emotional wounds. Pay attention to any signs of imbalance or discomfort and seek appropriate professional guidance for healing and support. Embrace self-care practices that nourish your body, mind, and soul. Engage in activities such as yoga, meditation, or spending time in nature to restore balance and promote inner harmony. The square aspect between the Sun and Neptune on May 3rd may create a sense of confusion or lack of clarity regarding your health. It's crucial to listen to your body's signals and trust your intuition. Avoid overexertion and prioritize rest and rejuvenation when needed. The conjunction between Venus and Chiron on May 21st invites you to focus on emotional healing and self-love. Nurture your emotional well-being by engaging in activities that bring you joy, surrounding yourself with positive influences, and seeking support from loved ones. Incorporate a balanced and nutritious diet into your routine, paying attention to any specific dietary needs or sensitivities. Maintain a regular exercise regimen that suits your preferences and supports overall well-being. Remember to find a healthy balance between work and personal life to avoid excessive stress or burnout. May is a month for self-care, healing, and embracing practices that promote overall well-being.

Travel

May offers favorable energies for travel and exploration for Libra. The conjunction between Venus and Uranus on May 18th ignites your adventurous spirit and may inspire spontaneous trips or unique experiences. Embrace opportunities to venture beyond your usual surroundings and expand your horizons. Whether it's a weekend getaway or a more extended journey, travel allows you to gain new perspectives, broaden your knowledge, and connect with diverse cultures. Pay attention to practical aspects of travel planning, such as budgeting, logistics, and safety precautions. The conjunction between Mercury and Uranus on May 31st enhances your communication skills and intellectual curiosity during your travels. Engage in meaningful conversations, interact with locals, and be open to new ideas and perspectives.

Embrace the spontaneity of travel while also being mindful of your personal boundaries and limitations. May supports your desire for exploration, self-discovery, and creating lasting memories through travel experiences.

Insight from the stars

May brings transformative energy for Libra, empowering personal growth, and enhancing your ability to communicate effectively. The celestial alignments encourage you to embrace change, explore new opportunities, and tap into your personal power. Take time for self-reflection, nurture your relationships, and prioritize self-care. Trust your intuition, listen to your body's signals, and make informed decisions. Approach conflicts with diplomacy and find common ground for resolution. May is a month of balance, transformation, and expansion. By aligning with the energies of the stars, you can navigate this period with grace and embrace the growth opportunities it presents.

Best days of the month: May 8th, 13th, 18th, 22nd, 23rd, 27th and 31st.

# June 2024

### Horoscope

In June, Libra, the cosmic energy encourages you to focus on your personal growth and relationships. The month begins with Mars forming a semi-sextile with Uranus on June 1st, inspiring you to embrace new ideas and explore exciting possibilities. This aspect encourages you to step out of your comfort zone and take calculated risks. The quintile aspects between the Sun and Neptune on June 1st and Venus and Neptune on June 2nd heighten your intuition and creativity, allowing you to tap into your artistic and spiritual side. Use this cosmic influence to engage in activities that nourish your soul and bring you joy.

### Love

June brings a harmonious energy to your love life, Libra. The conjunction between the Sun and Venus on June 4th enhances your charm, magnetism, and romantic appeal. It's a favorable time for new connections, deepening existing relationships, and expressing your affection openly. The sextile aspect between Venus and Chiron on June 11th encourages emotional healing and the resolution of any past wounds within relationships. Take this opportunity to have honest and compassionate conversations with your partner, fostering a deeper sense of understanding and intimacy.

For single Libras, the trine aspect between Mercury and Pluto on June 4th empowers you to attract potential partners who resonate with your authentic self. Trust your instincts and be open to exploring new connections. The square aspect between Venus and Saturn on June 8th may present some challenges or limitations within relationships. However, with patience, open communication, and a willingness to work through difficulties, you can overcome any obstacles and strengthen your bond.

Career

June brings favorable energy for career growth and professional endeavors, Libra. The conjunction between Mercury and Jupiter on June 4th enhances your communication skills and intellectual capabilities, making it an excellent time for negotiations, presentations, or expanding your network. This cosmic alignment supports your ability to express yourself with clarity and influence others with your ideas.

The sextile aspect between Mercury and Mars on June 21st boosts your productivity and allows you to tackle tasks with efficiency and determination. It's a favorable time to take the initiative, pursue new projects, or seek career advancements.

Finance

June brings a mixed bag of energies for your finances, Libra. The square aspect between Venus and Neptune on June 26th may bring some confusion or challenges when it comes to financial matters. It's crucial to exercise caution and avoid impulsive spending or making financial decisions based on unclear information. Take the time to review your financial plans, consult professionals if needed, and ensure that you have a clear understanding of your financial situation.

On a positive note, the trine aspect between Mercury and Saturn on June 26th supports your financial stability and long-term planning. It's an excellent time to create a budget, organize your financial documents, and implement strategies that promote financial security and growth. Remain disciplined and focused on your financial goals, and avoid unnecessary risks or investments.

Health

In June, it's essential for Libras to prioritize their health and well-being. The semi-sextile aspect between Mars and Neptune on June 8th highlights the need for balance between physical and emotional well-being. Engage in activities that promote relaxation, such as yoga, meditation, or spending time in nature. Pay attention to your body's signals and address any signs of imbalance promptly. Practice self-care, prioritize rest, and nourish your body with nutritious food.

The square aspect between Mercury and Chiron on June 28th may bring some emotional challenges or inner wounds to the surface. It's important to take the time to process and heal these emotions. Seek support from trusted friends, family, or a therapist if needed. Engaging in self-reflection and practicing self-compassion will contribute to your overall well-being.

### Travel

June offers opportunities for travel and exploration, Libra. The semi-sextile aspect between the Sun and Jupiter on June 28th ignites your sense of adventure and curiosity. If you have the chance, plan a getaway or explore new places within your local area. Traveling can provide you with valuable experiences, broaden your horizons, and rejuvenate your spirit.

Whether you embark on a physical journey or indulge in armchair travel through books and documentaries, use this time to expand your knowledge, connect with different cultures, and gain a fresh perspective on life.

### Insight from the stars

The celestial alignments in June emphasize the importance of balance, self-expression, and growth for Libra. Trust your intuition, embrace your unique qualities, and communicate your thoughts and feelings with clarity. Seek harmony in your relationships, both personal and professional, and approach challenges with patience and understanding. Take care of your physical and emotional well-being, and seize opportunities for personal and professional advancement. By aligning with the cosmic energies, you can navigate June with grace, authenticity, and a renewed sense of purpose.

Best days of the month: June 4th, 11th, 21st, 26th, 28th, 29th and 30th.

# July 2024

## Horoscope

In July 2024, Libra, the celestial movements bring a blend of dynamic energies that will shape your month. As a balanced and diplomatic sign, you may find yourself navigating unexpected changes and opportunities. This month calls for adaptability and open-mindedness as you embrace the ebb and flow of the astrological currents. While there may be challenges, remember that these are chances for personal growth and transformation. By staying grounded and maintaining your inner harmony, you can make the most of the energies at play.

## Love

The realm of love for Libra in July 2024 is marked by both harmonious and challenging aspects. The trine between Venus and Saturn on July 2nd fosters stability and commitment in your relationships. This alignment brings a deep sense of security and a desire to build a solid foundation with your partner. It's an excellent time to strengthen the bonds of love and deepen emotional connections.

However, on July 6th, the square between Venus and Chiron may bring up past wounds or insecurities. It's important to address these issues with compassion and open communication. Healing can occur when you're willing to confront and work through any unresolved issues. Seek support from your partner or a trusted confidant if needed.

Single Libras may also experience the effects of these aspects. The harmonious trine between Venus and Saturn may bring opportunities for a stable and enduring connection. Meanwhile, the square with Chiron encourages self-reflection and healing of past relationship wounds. Take this time to prioritize self-love and self-care, allowing yourself to fully heal before embarking on a new romantic journey.

Remember to be patient with yourself and your partner. Relationships require effort and understanding. Use the positive aspects to build a solid foundation, and address any challenges that arise with honesty and empathy. This will lead to deeper emotional connections and a stronger sense of love and harmony in your relationships.

## Career

In the realm of career, July 2024 presents various opportunities for growth and expansion for Libra. The quintile aspect between Mercury and Mars on July 1st enhances your communication skills and assertiveness. This alignment empowers you to express your ideas with confidence and make a lasting impression on colleagues and superiors. It's an ideal time to take the lead on projects, share your innovative thoughts, and showcase your abilities.

The sextile between Mercury and Jupiter on July 8th amplifies your intellectual capacity and presents favorable circumstances for professional development. You may find yourself engaged in fruitful collaborations, educational endeavors, or networking opportunities that broaden your horizons. This alignment encourages you to explore new avenues and expand your skill set. Embrace the chance to learn and acquire knowledge that will propel you forward in your career.

## Finance

July 2024 brings a mixed financial outlook for Libra. The trine between Venus and Saturn on July 2nd highlights the importance of stability and practicality in your financial matters. This alignment favors long-term planning, disciplined saving, and responsible decision-making. It's an opportune time to assess your financial goals and create a solid foundation for future prosperity.

However, the opposition between Venus and Pluto on July 12th suggests the need for caution when it comes to financial partnerships or joint ventures. Transparency and clear communication are essential to avoid any potential conflicts or misunderstandings. Conduct thorough research and seek professional advice before entering into any financial agreements.

Maintain a balanced approach to your finances throughout the month. While the positive aspects provide stability and growth opportunities, remain cautious and diligent in your financial dealings. Budgeting, careful planning, and mindful spending will contribute to your long-term financial security.

Health

The month of July urges Libra to prioritize their well-being and maintain a balanced approach to health. The opposition between Mercury and Pluto on July 3rd may bring mental and emotional challenges. It's essential to take time for self-reflection and identify any deep-rooted patterns or limiting beliefs that may be affecting your overall well-being. Seek support from trusted friends, family members, or professionals to help you navigate these internal struggles.

The square between the Sun and Chiron on July 15th may impact your vitality and energy levels. It's crucial to maintain a balanced lifestyle, incorporating regular exercise, proper nutrition, and sufficient rest into your routine. Pay attention to your emotional well-being as well. Engage in activities that promote relaxation, stress reduction, and self-care. Taking care of your mental and physical health will allow you to navigate the challenges of the month more effectively.

Travel

July offers opportunities for travel and exploration for Libra. The sextile between Venus and Uranus on July 8th may bring unexpected travel opportunities or spontaneous adventures. Embrace these experiences as they can lead to personal growth and enrich your perspective. Allow yourself to step out of your comfort zone and embrace new cultures, ideas, and environments.

However, be mindful of the square between Mercury and Uranus on July 21st, which may disrupt travel plans or create communication challenges. It's advisable to have contingency plans in place and maintain open lines of communication with travel companions or organizers. Adaptability and flexibility will be key during this time. Remember to prioritize safety and be prepared for any unforeseen circumstances.

Insight from the stars

The celestial influences in July 2024 urge you, Libra, to find balance within yourself and in your relationships. Embrace the unexpected changes and challenges as opportunities for growth and transformation. Trust your intuition and maintain an open mind as you navigate through this dynamic month. Remember to prioritize self-care and seek support when needed. With patience, adaptability, and a positive mindset, you can overcome any obstacles and achieve harmony in all aspects of your life.

Best days of the month: July 2nd, 8th, 10th, 15th, 18th, 21st and 30th.

# August 2024

## Horoscope

In August 2024, Libra, the astrological aspects present a month of self-discovery, growth, and dynamic energy. The celestial movements urge you to embrace your individuality and assert your desires while maintaining your natural harmony and diplomacy. This month offers opportunities for personal and professional development, as well as the chance to deepen your relationships and explore new experiences. By tapping into your inner wisdom and maintaining balance, you can navigate the month with grace and fulfillment.

## Love

For Libra, the realm of love in August 2024 is marked by a mix of intense aspects and harmonious alignments. The sextile between Mars and True Node on August 1st ignites passion and sparks a deep connection in your relationships. This alignment brings opportunities for emotional growth and aligning your desires with your partner's.

However, the square between Venus and Uranus on August 2nd may bring unexpected changes or disruptions in your love life. It's crucial to remain open-minded and flexible during this time. Embrace the opportunity to break free from old patterns and explore new ways of expressing your love and affection.

For single Libras, the quintile between Venus and Jupiter on August 2nd brings a sense of adventure and optimism in your search for love. Be open to new experiences and connections, as they may lead to unexpected romantic opportunities.

Remember to communicate openly and honestly with your partner or potential love interests. The conjunction between Mercury and Venus on August 7th enhances your communication skills, allowing you to express your emotions and desires with clarity and authenticity.

### Career

In the realm of career, August 2024 presents a mix of challenges and opportunities for Libra. The conjunction between Mars and Jupiter on August 14th brings a surge of energy and enthusiasm, propelling you toward ambitious goals and professional success.

This alignment empowers you to take bold steps, make important decisions, and embrace leadership roles.

However, the square between the Sun and Saturn on August 10th may present obstacles or delays in your career path. It's essential to remain patient and resilient, knowing that challenges can lead to valuable lessons and personal growth. Stay focused on your long-term goals and persevere through any setbacks.

Seek collaborations and partnerships that align with your values and support your professional aspirations. The biquintile aspect between Venus and Chiron on August 19th encourages you to seek mentors or advisors who can provide guidance and help you navigate challenges.

Finance

August 2024 brings a focus on financial stability and responsible decision-making for Libra. The trine between Venus and Pluto on August 29th highlights opportunities for financial transformation and empowerment. This alignment encourages you to reevaluate your financial goals, assess your investments, and make strategic decisions that lead to long-term prosperity.

However, the quincunx aspects between Venus and Neptune on August 4th and Venus and Saturn on August 19th call for caution and careful planning in financial matters. Avoid impulsive spending or risky investments during these times. Instead, focus on creating a solid financial foundation through budgeting, saving, and making informed choices.

Health

In August 2024, Libra's well-being demands attention and self-care. The sesquiquadrate aspects between the Sun and Neptune on August 6th and the Sun and Chiron on August 30th may affect your energy levels and emotional well-being. It's essential to prioritize self-care practices that nurture your body, mind, and soul.

Engage in activities that promote relaxation, such as meditation, yoga, or spending time in nature. Take care of your emotional health by nurturing positive relationships and seeking support when needed. Pay attention to your energy levels and ensure you are getting sufficient rest and sleep. Remember that self-care is not selfish but necessary for your overall well-being.

### Travel

August offers opportunities for travel and exploration for Libra. The biquintile aspect between Mercury and Neptune on August 23rd enhances your intuition and opens doors to new adventures. Embrace these opportunities for personal growth and cultural enrichment. Whether it's a spontaneous weekend getaway or a long-awaited vacation, allow yourself to explore new horizons and create lasting memories.

### Insight from the stars

The celestial influences in August 2024 urge you, Libra, to embrace your individuality, communicate authentically, and pursue your passions with determination. Trust your intuition and tap into your diplomatic nature to navigate any challenges that come your way. By maintaining balance in all aspects of your life and embracing self-care, you can find harmony and fulfillment. Remember that your journey is unique, and by honoring your true self, you can shine brightly and make a positive impact on those around you.

Best days of the month: August 1st, 7th, 14th, 19th, 23rd, 29th and 30th

## September 2024

### Horoscope

Welcome to September, dear Libra! As the autumn season begins, the celestial energies align to bring you a month of profound self-discovery, balanced relationships, and personal growth. You will have the opportunity to dive deep into your emotions, establish harmonious connections, and find equilibrium in various aspects of your life. This transformative period calls for introspection, open communication, and a willingness to embrace both challenges and opportunities that come your way. By staying true to your authentic self and fostering genuine connections with others, you can navigate this month with grace and create a solid foundation for future success.

### Love

In matters of the heart, September 2024 holds the potential for profound emotional connections and the deepening of existing relationships. The opposition between Venus and the True Node on September 3rd illuminates the significance of balancing your desires with the needs and aspirations of your partner. This alignment urges you to delve into the depths of your emotions and cultivate a sense of authenticity and vulnerability in your relationships.

For single Libras, this month may bring unexpected encounters and romantic opportunities. Keep your heart open and be receptive to the energies around you. The trine between Venus and Jupiter on September 15th creates a magnetic and expansive atmosphere for love, encouraging you to step outside your comfort zone and embrace new romantic possibilities.

Career

September presents favorable aspects for career growth and professional development for Libra. The square between Mars and Neptune on September 3rd may temporarily cloud your career path with confusion or ambiguity. However, this is an opportunity to trust your intuition and seek clarity before making any major decisions. Take the time to reassess your goals, align your actions with your long-term aspirations, and embrace a flexible mindset.

The biquintile aspect between Mercury and Pluto on September 12th enhances your analytical and problem-solving abilities, allowing you to overcome obstacles and find innovative solutions in your professional endeavors. Collaboration and teamwork may play a significant role in your success this month. Embrace opportunities to work with others, as they can lead to remarkable advancements in your career.

Finance

In terms of finances, September requires diligent planning and practical decision-making for Libra. The opposition between Venus and Chiron on September 16th may trigger insecurities or emotional patterns related to money. It's crucial to address any limiting beliefs surrounding abundance and cultivate a healthy mindset towards prosperity. Seek support from financial advisors or trusted friends to optimize your resources and make informed decisions.

The trine aspect between Venus and Jupiter on September 15th brings a potential for financial expansion and growth. Consider exploring new investment opportunities or seeking advice on long-term financial planning. This alignment invites you to trust in the abundance of the universe and take calculated risks when it comes to your financial well-being.

## Health

September places a strong emphasis on self-care and emotional well-being for Libra. The sesquiquadrate aspect between the Sun and Pluto on September 6th may intensify emotions and create added stress. It's essential to prioritize self-reflection, engage in relaxation techniques, and seek support when needed. Nurturing positive relationships, maintaining a balanced lifestyle, and finding healthy outlets for stress management are key to your overall well-being during this period.

Make self-care rituals a daily practice and pay attention to your mental and emotional health. Engaging in activities such as meditation, journaling, or seeking professional guidance can assist you in navigating any challenges that arise.

## Travel

September offers opportunities for travel and exploration, allowing you to expand your horizons and broaden your perspective. The trine between the Sun and Uranus on September 19th brings a sense of adventure and excitement to your travel endeavors.

Whether it's a spontaneous weekend getaway or a planned trip, embrace the opportunity to explore new environments and immerse yourself in different cultures. These experiences will not only provide relaxation but also deepen your understanding of the world and enrich your personal growth.

Insight from the stars

As you move through September 2024, the celestial influences invite you to find balance within yourself and your relationships. Embrace your authentic self, communicate openly, and trust your intuition. This transformative period calls for deep introspection, personal growth, and the cultivation of harmonious connections. By embracing the transformative energies of the month, you can navigate challenges with grace, discover new avenues for personal and professional fulfillment, and lay a solid foundation for a brighter future.

Best days of the month: September 3rd, 12th, 15th, 19th, 22nd, 25th and 30th

# October 2024

### Horoscope

Welcome to the transformative and enchanting month of October, dear Libra! As the autumn leaves paint the world with vibrant hues, the cosmic energies beckon you to embark on a profound journey of self-discovery and balance. This month, the celestial alignments cast a gentle spotlight on your inner world, urging you to delve deep into your emotions, seek harmony in your relationships, and embrace the transformative power of introspection. By embracing these cosmic invitations, you can pave the way for personal growth, forge authentic connections, and create a solid foundation for a future filled with love, success, and fulfillment.

### Love

Throughout October, the cosmos weaves a tapestry of emotional depth and passionate connections in your love life, dear Libra. The sesquiquadrate aspect between Venus and Neptune on October 3rd evokes a sense of soulful yearning and spiritual alignment within romantic relationships. It is a time to dive fearlessly into the depths of your emotions, to open up to vulnerability, and to explore the uncharted territories of intimacy with your partner. This alignment emphasizes the importance of trust, compassion, and authentic expression of your deepest desires.

For single Libras, this month brings forth a serendipitous dance of chance encounters and magnetic attractions. The trine between Venus and Mars on October 8th sets the stage for passionate connections and exciting romantic possibilities. Allow your desires to take flight, embrace the enchantment of the moment, and let your intuition guide you towards unexpected love interests. The universe is conspiring to bring you closer to your heart's true desires.

Career

October presents a celestial symphony of growth and advancement in your professional endeavors, dear Libra. The square aspect between Mercury and Mars on October 6th may introduce temporary challenges or conflicts in the workplace. However, do not be disheartened, for within these seemingly daunting hurdles lie opportunities for personal growth and professional triumph. Embrace the fires of assertiveness, tap into your inner diplomatic prowess, and communicate your ideas with clarity and confidence. By doing so, you can rise above any adversity and emerge as a beacon of inspiration for your colleagues and superiors.

The trine between Mercury and Jupiter on October 8th bestows upon you the gift of eloquence, expanded horizons, and exciting collaborations. This alignment amplifies your communication skills, encouraging you to share your insights, forge new connections, and explore avenues for professional growth. Be open to networking opportunities and engage in meaningful conversations with like-minded individuals. The seeds you plant during this fertile period have the potential to blossom into fruitful partnerships and rewarding ventures.

Finance

October calls for a mindful and discerning approach to your finances, dear Libra. The quincunx aspect between Venus and Jupiter on October 10th urges you to reevaluate your financial decisions and reassess your long-term goals. Take a step back, review your financial strategies, and ensure they are in alignment with your aspirations. Exercise caution against impulsive spending and seek expert advice when needed. This period demands meticulous planning, budgeting, and a conscious effort to strike a balance between your desires and your financial responsibilities.

However, the cosmos bestows its blessings upon you as well. The trine between Venus and Saturn on October 4th and the sextile between Venus and Pluto on October 17th infuse stability and potential for financial growth. These alignments serve as celestial anchors, grounding your financial endeavors and providing fertile ground for long-term investments or ventures. Embrace a prudent approach, harness your innate diplomatic skills when making financial decisions, and consider strategies that align with your long-term financial security.

Health

In October, the cosmos places a loving emphasis on your well-being, urging you to prioritize self-care, emotional balance, and holistic nourishment, dear Libra. The sesquiquadrate aspect between the Sun and Chiron on October 4th invites you to delve into the depths of your emotional wounds and embark on a journey of healing. Take time to reflect, acknowledge your vulnerabilities, and seek the support of trusted confidants or professionals if needed. Emotional well-being forms the foundation of your overall health, and addressing any lingering wounds allows for profound transformation and growth.

The quincunx aspect between Mercury and Uranus on October 11th encourages you to explore alternative healing modalities, embrace mindfulness practices, and expand your knowledge of holistic well-being. Embrace the power of meditation, yoga, or other forms of spiritual practices that resonate with your soul. Nurture your body through wholesome nutrition, regular exercise, and restorative sleep. Remember to find balance between your social engagements and the need for solitude, allowing yourself ample time for introspection and rejuvenation.

Travel

October brings opportunities for captivating and transformative travel experiences, dear Libra. As the Sun quincunxes Uranus on October 19th, unexpected travel invitations or spontaneous adventures may come your way. Embrace the spirit of wanderlust and allow yourself to step outside of your comfort zone. Whether it's a solo pilgrimage to a spiritual retreat or an exciting group excursion, trust the universe's guidance and embrace the opportunities that unfold before you. These journeys hold the potential for personal growth, new perspectives, and profound connections with fellow travelers.

Insight from the stars

Dear Libra, as you embark on the cosmic dance of October, the celestial energies invite you to surrender to the transformative power of self-discovery, balance, and harmony. Embrace the depths of your emotions, nurture your relationships, and engage in meaningful introspection. By aligning your actions with your authentic desires, you pave the way for personal growth, profound connections, and a future filled with love, success, and fulfillment.

Best days of the month: October 8th, 13th, 17th, 22nd, 24th, 26th, and 30th.

# November 2024

### Horoscope

Dear Libra, as the autumn season deepens and the leaves fall gracefully, November brings forth a transformative and expansive energy into your life. This month holds the promise of personal growth, introspection, and harmonious relationships. The cosmic alignments invite you to explore new horizons, embrace the depths of your emotions, and embark on a profound journey of self-discovery.

The celestial dance in November encourages you to delve into your inner world, examine your beliefs and values, and align them with your authentic self. It's a time for reflection, introspection, and finding your center amidst the ever-changing external circumstances. By embracing this introspective energy, you can gain a deeper understanding of yourself, paving the way for personal growth and self-realization.

## Love

Throughout November, the cosmos weaves a tapestry of emotional depth and transformative experiences in your love life, dear Libra. The opposition between Venus and Jupiter on November 3rd evokes a sense of magnetic attraction and growth within your relationships. This alignment encourages you to expand your horizons, engage in meaningful conversations, and open yourself up to new perspectives. Single Libras may find themselves drawn to individuals who inspire them intellectually and share their thirst for exploration.

The trine between Venus and Chiron on November 3rd brings healing and understanding to the forefront of your romantic connections. This aspect invites you to embrace vulnerability, communicate your needs, and foster a safe and nurturing environment for emotional growth within your partnerships. It's a time for deepening the bond and finding solace in the comfort of your loved one's presence.

## Career

November presents opportunities for professional growth and advancement, dear Libra. The trine between Mercury and Mars on November 2nd energizes your communication skills, making it an ideal time for negotiations, presentations, or collaborative projects. Your words carry a powerful impact, allowing you to assert your ideas with confidence and clarity. Utilize your diplomatic abilities to foster harmonious working relationships and find innovative solutions to any challenges that arise.

The sextile between Mercury and Pluto on November 2nd empowers you with insight and strategic thinking. This alignment encourages you to delve deep into your work, uncover hidden potentials, and make transformative changes that have a lasting impact. Embrace your natural ability to analyze and synthesize information, and trust your instincts when it comes to making important decisions. Your discerning approach sets the stage for success in your professional endeavors.

Finance

In November, the cosmos calls for a balanced and mindful approach to your finances, dear Libra. The square aspect between Venus and Neptune on November 9th urges you to exercise caution and discernment when it comes to financial decisions. Be wary of potential illusions or unrealistic promises. Take the time to review your financial strategies, seek expert advice if needed, and ensure that your investments align with your long-term goals. A practical and grounded approach will help you navigate through any uncertainties.

However, the sextile between Venus and Saturn on November 22nd bestows stability and potential for financial growth. This alignment invites you to cultivate a strong work ethic, exercise prudence in your spending habits, and embrace responsible financial management. By prioritizing discipline and long-term security, you can lay the groundwork for financial stability and abundance.

### Health

November emphasizes the importance of self-care and holistic well-being, dear Libra. The sesquiquadrate aspect between the Sun and Neptune on November 4th calls for balance between your physical, emotional, and spiritual needs. Take time for self-reflection, engage in activities that bring you joy and peace, and nurture your inner world. Practice mindfulness, meditation, or other relaxation techniques to alleviate stress and restore your overall well-being.

The trine between the Sun and Saturn on November 4th provides a solid foundation for establishing healthy routines and habits. Embrace regular exercise, balanced nutrition, and restorative sleep. Pay attention to your emotional state, seeking support and guidance when needed. By nurturing your mind, body, and spirit, you can enhance your overall health and vitality, enabling you to navigate the month with strength and resilience.

Travel

November offers opportunities for transformative and enriching travel experiences, dear Libra. The Sun's sextile to Pluto on November 21st brings forth a sense of adventure and the potential for deep transformation through travel. Consider exploring new cultures, immersing yourself in spiritual retreats, or embarking on nature-based journeys that allow you to reconnect with your inner self. These experiences have the power to expand your horizons, provide fresh perspectives, and ignite a renewed sense of purpose.

# COMPLETE LIBRA 2024 PERSONAL HOROSCOPE

Insight from the stars

Dear Libra, as you embrace the cosmic energies of November, the celestial alignments guide you towards transformative growth, harmonious relationships, and a deeper understanding of yourself and others. By nurturing your emotional well-being, embracing balance in your professional endeavors, and cultivating mindful financial habits, you can pave the way for a month filled with personal and professional fulfillment. Trust the wisdom of the stars as you navigate through the transformative energies, and allow the universe to guide you towards love, success, and inner harmony.

Best days of the month: November 2nd, 7th, 11th, 18th, 20th, 23rd, and 30th

# December 2024

## Horoscope

As we step into the final month of the year, December holds immense significance and transformative potential for you, dear Libra. The cosmic energies align to support your journey of self-discovery, personal growth, and manifestation. This month marks a pivotal time for reflection, introspection, and setting intentions for the upcoming year. The celestial alignments inspire you to delve deep within, uncover hidden truths, and align your actions with your authentic self. Embrace this period of self-reflection, for it will pave the way for a remarkable start to the new year. Trust the process and have faith in your innate abilities as you navigate the path ahead.

## Love

In matters of the heart, December brings a potent blend of passion, harmony, and self-discovery for you, dear Libra. The planetary configurations infuse your love life with heightened emotions, deep connections, and transformative experiences. With Venus biquintile

Jupiter on December 1st, love and romance take center stage, creating an atmosphere of optimism, joy, and expanded possibilities. This celestial alignment encourages you to embrace love's adventures, express your affection, and foster meaningful connections. If you're single, this is an opportune time to meet potential partners who possess the qualities you desire. For those already in a relationship, this period offers a chance to deepen your bond, rekindle the flame of passion, and embark on new adventures together. Embrace the energy of love, and let it guide you towards fulfilling and harmonious relationships.

Career

December presents abundant opportunities for growth, recognition, and professional advancement, dear Libra. The dynamic interplay between celestial energies propels your career aspirations forward and encourages you to seize the spotlight. The opposition between Mercury and Jupiter on December 4th amplifies your intellectual prowess, persuasive communication skills, and strategic thinking. This cosmic alignment empowers you to showcase your abilities, take on new challenges, and engage in negotiations that can propel your career to new heights.

Trust in your talents, believe in your ideas, and step into the limelight with confidence. However, it's essential to navigate the potential obstacles that may arise. The Sun's square aspect with Saturn on December 4th may introduce temporary setbacks or challenges. But with your tenacity and resilience, you can overcome these hurdles and emerge stronger than before. Embrace a proactive mindset, seek innovative solutions, and maintain a harmonious balance between ambition and responsibility. By harnessing these energies, you can make significant strides in your professional pursuits.

Finance

December invites you to adopt a balanced and prudent approach to your finances, dear Libra. The celestial configurations emphasize the importance of responsible financial management and mindful decision-making. While the holiday season may tempt you to indulge in splurges, it's crucial to maintain a realistic perspective and stick to a well-thought-out budget. The semi square between Venus and Saturn on December 5th reminds you to exercise restraint and discipline in your spending habits. This alignment encourages you to prioritize long-term financial stability over short-term gratification. It's an opportune time to assess your financial goals, reevaluate your investment strategies, and make necessary adjustments to ensure a solid foundation for the future. Seek wise counsel, explore new avenues for income generation, and focus on building a sustainable financial framework. Remember, small steps taken now can lead to significant financial gains in the future. By embracing a balanced approach to your finances, you can navigate the month of December with financial confidence and stability.

Health

In December, your well-being takes center stage, dear Libra. The celestial energies inspire you to prioritize self-care, nurture your body, and cultivate inner harmony. With the Sun's trine to Chiron on December 10th, a profound healing energy permeates your being, facilitating physical, emotional, and spiritual wellness. This alignment encourages you to address any lingering health concerns, adopt holistic practices, and engage in activities that promote balance and vitality. Take time for self-reflection, establish a self-care routine, and prioritize rest and rejuvenation.

It's crucial to strike a harmonious balance between work and personal life to prevent burnout. Embrace mindfulness practices, such as meditation or yoga, to enhance your overall well-being. Nourish your body with wholesome foods, stay hydrated, and engage in regular physical exercise to maintain vitality and strengthen your immune system. Remember to listen to your body's cues and make self-care a non-negotiable priority. By tending to your well-being, you can navigate the month of December with renewed energy, vitality, and emotional resilience.

Travel

December presents exciting opportunities for travel and exploration, dear Libra. The celestial alignments open doors to new experiences, cultural enrichment, and adventure. Whether it's a short getaway or an extended journey, the cosmos encourages you to embrace the spirit of exploration and expand your horizons. With the Sun's biquintile to Mars on December 20th, your adventurous spirit is ignited, inspiring you to seek novel experiences and immerse yourself in different cultures. This alignment infuses your travels with enthusiasm, vitality, and a zest for life. Plan your trips mindfully, allowing for spontaneous detours and serendipitous encounters along the way. Engage in activities that broaden your perspective, connect you with different traditions, and offer opportunities for personal growth. Whether you're embarking on a solo adventure or traveling with loved ones, December promises to be a transformative and enriching time. Embrace the joy of exploration, embrace new cultures, and create lasting memories that will shape your worldview.

Insight from the stars

December brings forth a cosmic symphony of transformative energies, dear Libra. The celestial alignments encourage you to embark on a journey of self-discovery, embrace love's adventures, seize professional opportunities, and prioritize your well-being. Trust in the wisdom of the universe, listen to your intuition, and align your actions with your deepest aspirations. This month offers a profound opportunity for personal growth, paving the way for a remarkable start to the new year. Embrace the transformative energies of December and allow the stars to guide you towards a path of fulfillment, harmony, and success.

Best days of the month: December 2nd, 10th, 19th, 21st, 23rd, 28th and 31st.

Printed in Great Britain
by Amazon